Like the Countless Raindrops

RICKY CLEMONS

PUBLISHED BY FIDELI PUBLISHING, INC.

ISBN: 978-1-955622-16-5

Published by

Fideli Publishing, Inc.
119 W. Morgan St.
Martinsville, IN 46151
www.FideliPublishing.com

Table of Contents

Like the Countless Raindrops

God's love is like the countless raindrops falling down on the deepest ocean.

God's mercy is like the countless raindrops falling down on the highest mountain top.

God's truth is like the countless raindrops falling down on the dense forest.

God's wisdom is like the countless raindrops falling down on the most beautiful countryside.

God's grace is like the countless raindrops falling down on the most crowded city.

God's faithfulness is like the countless raindrops falling down on the most beautiful house.

God's forgiveness is like the countless raindrops falling down on the biggest forest fire.

God's victories are like the countless raindrops falling down on the tallest building.

God's salvation is like the countless raindrops falling down on every living soul.

God the Father, God the Son and God the Holy Spirit is like the countless raindrops falling down on you and me to cool our hearts down from the devil's scorching-hot sins that can't dry up God's love for us.

God's presence is all around us like the countless raindrops falling down all around us.

God's judgment is like the countless raindrops falling down on everyone who ever lived and is alive today to be completely transparent before God who will judge everybody right and fair with no prejudices.

It can rain for days and cause a big flood upon the land and that is not good for you and me, but the spiritual raindrops of God's will can flood the devil's temptations so they will not be more on us than what we can bear.

People will be lost in sin because of their own free will in choosing to rebel against God, who has limited the devil's power so it won't flood our souls with his sins.

We can flood our own souls with selfish desires that can be like the countless raindrops of our free will choices.

It's Nothing New Today

Many children being killed is nothing new today.

Back in the Bible days, King Pharaoh ordered all the Hebrew baby boys to be killed.

It seemed to be that only the baby Moses was saved from being killed.

It's nothing new today that many little children are being killed by the devil's human agents.

Little children are so very innocent every day and they are not mature enough to make sensible choices.

Little children must be taught by adults to do right.

A lot of parents are teaching their little children to do bad things and God will hold the parents accountable for their children's bad behavior.

Back in the Bible days, King Herod gave the order to kill all the baby boys who were two years old or younger.

It seemed to be that only the baby Jesus was safe from being killed.

King Pharaoh and King Herod were two evil kings who caused many parents to grieve over the deaths of their baby boys.

The kings couldn't care less about their grieving.

It's the same way today, with murderers of little children because they don't care about mothers and fathers grieving over the deaths of their little children.

It's nothing new today that many people love to kill little innocent children just like hunting to shoot down a deer.

Every little child who has been killed will grow up in heaven when Jesus Christ comes back again to give them eternal life.

All of you grieving parents need to get your souls right with the Lord who will save you from your sins so that you can all one day see your children again in heaven.

Your deceased children are saved in Jesus and will go to heaven, but you will be lost and miss out on heaven if you don't believe in Jesus and don't love Jesus and keep His Commandments.

It's a terrible sin against God to murder anyone, but when people murder little children it greatly grieves God's heart.

Deceased little immature children will surely inherit the kingdom of God, but their mothers and fathers who are still alive must be saved in Jesus Christ to be able to be with their children in heaven one day.

Little children's calling is very sure in God.

You and I must choose to make our calling very sure in God.

It's nothing new today that many little children are being killed all around the world but God will get vengeance, especially on murderers of little children.

Real, True Beauty

Real, true beauty is beautiful words and beautiful actions beyond the beauty of the skin.

Real, true beauty is a beautiful mind that will think on the Lord.

Real, true beauty is beautiful words that will speak about the Lord.

Real, true beauty is beautiful actions that will do what the Lord says in His holy word.

The beauty of the skin will fade away in old age wrinkles.

The real, true beauty of words about the Lord will never grow old.

Real, true beauty is beneath the beauty of the skin.

A burning fire can destroy the beauty of the skin, but not the beauty of words and actions.

Bad chemicals can destroy the beauty of the skin, but not the beauty of words and actions that will surely get the attention of our Lord Jesus Christ, who spoke the most beautiful words and had the most beautiful actions when He lived His life without sin in this sinful world.

Jesus spoke the truth and those were the most beautiful words to speak.

Jesus live the truth and those were the most beautiful actions to live.

Jesus had the most beautiful mind when He lived on earth without sin.

Jesus Had the most beautiful heart when he lived on earth without sin.

The beauty of the skin will never be more beautiful than a beautiful mind.

The beauty of the skin will never be more beautiful than beautiful words.

The beauty of the skin will never be more beautiful than beautiful actions.

The beauty of the skin will never be more beautiful than a beautiful heart.

A beautiful woman can truly thank the Lord for giving her outward beauty, but a woman should never forget that the Lord can take her beauty away from her if she doesn't give Him the glory and praise for her beauty.

Real, true beauty is a beautiful character being about the Lord who is the origin of inner beauty and outer beauty.

A woman will look so rich in her outward beauty, but her inner beauty is spiritual riches that will never fade away.

A woman who has both inward beauty and outward beauty seems to be rare in this world today.

The Hard Realities

Every day we must live with a hard reality that some things are not what we want them to be in our lives.

Everybody lives with some kind of hard reality and many people don't want to face up to this with a sober mind.

Many people use drugs to help them cope with the hard realities in their lives.

Many people use alcohol to help them cope with the hard realities in their lives.

Many people use manipulation to help them cope with the hard realities in their lives.

Many people use food to help them cope with the hard realities in their lives.

Many people go on shopping sprees to help them cope with the hard realities in their lives.

Many people will come up with some kind of way to help them cope with the hard realities in their lives.

Many people will try everything else to help them to cope, except giving Jesus Christ a try to help them cope with the hard realities in their lives.

Jesus came to this world and He had to face up to the hard realities of being spit on, beaten, bruised and being nailed on the cross to save you and me from the hard realities of being lost in our sins.

It's sin that brings on us the hard realities that Jesus got the victory over because He never sinned against God.

It is only through Jesus Christ that you and I can get the victory over our hard realities in life because they are never too hard for Jesus because He always prayed to God and obeyed God who gave Him the strength to cope with the hard realities of saving us from our sins.

We Can Think

We can think before we say something wrong.

We can think before we do something wrong.

Animals don't have a mind to think at all.

Animals will do things with their fixed pattern behavior.

Animals can't think before they do something.

You and I can think before we do something because God gave us a mind to think with.

We can train animals to do things, but they can't think on doing anything themselves.

You and I can think on what we want to do.

We have a mind to think even on the spur of the moment when we can think to make a split-second decision to not say and not do something wrong.

We can think before we put our words into actions, whether those actions are good or bad, because God gave us a free will choice to choose to think before we say something and before we do something.

If we don't say one word, we can think before we do something.

If we are blind and couldn't see, we can think before we say something and before we do something.

If we are paralyzed, we can think before we say something.

If we can't hear, we can think before we do something.

God gave us all a mind to think once, twice or many more times before we say something and before we do something, whether that something is good or bad.

Even someone who is sick in the mind can think before saying something delusional and doing something delusional.

Many people who are sick in the mind can think and know that they are not an animal.

We can think, no matter where we live around the world, because God gave us human beings a mind to think as much as we want to think before we say something and before we do something.

The choices that we make come from what we think in our minds.

Even many delusional people can think and make plans to hurt people and kill people and have a delusional belief that they are on a mission from God.

God created the mind to be powerful to think on good things and to do good things without us always having to think twice about it.

People who are addicted to drugs can think, even though what they're thinking might be far from what is good and right for them.

There are people who are so ill that they can't think about anything, but the Lord has His good doctors to give them good medicine to help them think again before saying something and before doing something.

For Only a Moment

There are people who we see for only a moment and we never see them again for the rest of our lives.

There are people who we only talk to once in life and it's like only a moment that passes by and never comes back again.

We had loved ones in our lives who were only in our lives for a moment, but they will always be in our minds even though they've now gone to the grave of no return.

We drive by many people on the road for only a moment and we don't know if we will see them driving on the road ever again.

We see some people in the grocery store for only a moment and we don't know if we will see some of those people in the grocery store ever again.

We see some people in the doctor's office for only a moment and we don't know if we will see those people in the doctor's office ever again.

Life passes by like only a moment that doesn't last long at all, but Jesus Christ is coming back again one day soon to take us to heaven if we are saved in Him.

It will be like only a moment that we will be changed from mortal to immortality and the angels will take us up on the clouds of glory to be with Jesus up in the sky.

There are people who come into our lives for only a moment, like a visitor in church.

He or she might never come back again and we just don't know if they are alive or dead.

Life in this world is for only a moment and we need to live our moment loving Jesus Christ and keeping His commandments that are eternal beyond everybody's moment in life.

Only Jesus can truly turn our moment in life into eternal life when He comes back again, which will be like only a moment to God in heaven.

There are so many people who we will see for only a moment but hopefully we will see many of those people in heaven when Jesus Christ comes back again to be beyond everyone's moment in time.

We All Can Be Slow

There are people who are slow in catching onto things, but they are not stupid to know if we treat them good or bad.

You and I can be slow in catching onto things when it comes to Jesus, who knows how to work out everything for our good.

We can be slow to listen to and obey the voice of God's Holy Spirit telling us to say this and not say that.

We can be slow to listen to and obey the voice of God's Holy Spirit telling us to do this and not do that.

We all can be slow when it comes to loving everybody like Jesus loves everybody.

Jesus gave up His life on the cross to save everybody from their sins.

Jesus is not slow to answer our prayers and He always answers on time and not too slow or too fast.

Jesus is not slow to provide all of our needs, whatever they might be.

Jesus will provide everything to us on time.

There are people who are slow in learning things, but they are not stupid and know if you and I love them or don't love them.

You and I can be slow when it comes to trusting Jesus to work things out for us according to His holy will.

We all can be slow in catching onto the spiritual things of the Lord, who can send angels unaware to us who surely won't even know it because we are spiritually slow and don't recognize God's messengers from heaven.

We all can be slow in having faith as big as a mustard seed that we can stop from growing into a beautiful fruit tree for doubting what Jesus can do for us.

Back in the Bible days, the religious leaders and Pharisees believed that they were fast to try to trap Jesus into saying something wrong, but they were slow to trap Jesus who was very fast to stay ahead of them because he knew their hearts before they spoke one word to Him.

One Man

One man can build up a nation.

One man can ruin a nation.

One man can start a conspiracy.

One man can deceive millions of people.

One man can start a war.

One man can end a war.

One man can rock the world.

One man can lead the nation.

One man can oppress a nation.

One man can spread a lie around the world.

One man can cause a nation to be in debt.

One man can ruin a military operation.

One man can find a cure for a deadly disease.

One man can cheat millions of people.

One man can corrupt the government.

One man can corrupt millions of people.

One man can give encouragement to millions of people.

One man can kill millions of people.

One man has brought sin into all the world.

One sinless man has redeemed the world back to God.

One man can change the whole world.

One man can cause a woman to hate all men.

One man can cause a woman to not trust any man.

One man can cause a woman to feel on top of the world.

One man can cause a woman to feel like she is the most beautiful woman in the world.

One man can cheer up millions of people.

One man can discourage millions of people.

One man found grace in the eyes of God to spare his life and his family and some animals from the flood that covered over the whole world.

One sinless man got the victory over death and the grave.

One sinless man has a heaven to put us in.

Worthy is the Lamb of God

O Lord, I deserve to have my back lashed a hundred or more times.

O Lord, I deserve to be spit on one hundred times.

O Lord, you didn't deserve to get lashes on your back.

O Lord, you didn't deserve to be spit on.

O Lord, I deserve to have 100 bruises on my head.

O Lord I deserve to bleed my blood all over my body.

O Lord, you didn't deserve to get bruises on your head.

O Lord, you didn't deserve to bleed any blood.

O Lord, you did it all for me as if I was the only sinner who You want to save from my sins.

O Lord, I deserve to have nail prints in my hands.

O Lord, I deserve to have nail prints in my feet.

O Lord, you didn't deserve to get nail prints in your hands.

O Lord, you didn't deserve to get nail prints in your feet.

O Lord, you did it all for me, who deserves to die and be lost in my sins.

Worthy is the Lamb of God is You, my Lord and Savior Jesus Christ.

I can shed a million tears for all that you've done for me, O Lord, and it doesn't come close to how you felt in the Garden of Gethsemane where you, O Lord, had sweat so very intense to look like drops of blood dripping down from your face.

You knew, O Lord, that the cup of God's wrath was so bitter for you to drink in my place.

Worthy is the Lamb of God, is You, my Lord and Savior Jesus Christ, who had left all of heaven and given up all of your riches to come to this sinful world to save a poor sinner like me and one day give me Your eternal riches and wealth of eternal life.

If our Lord and Savior Jesus Christ had not laid down His life for the sins of all the world, then Enoch would have had to leave heaven and go to the grave.

If Jesus had not laid down His life on the cross for the sins of all the world, then Moses would have had to leave heaven and go to the grave.

If Jesus had not died on the cross and risen again, then Elijah would have had to leave heaven and go to the grave because he was not more worthy than Jesus, who created the heavens and earth.

Worthy is the Lamb of God, is Jesus Christ, who humbled Himself like a lamb before the religious leaders and Pharisees and before the Roman soldiers who were like hungry wolves waiting to devour Jesus.

Jesus held back all of His power to become like a helpless little lamb to be preyed upon by the hungry wild beast called the devil, who along with his human agents, could not tempt Jesus to sin against God.

Jesus was the lamb who heard and answered His master God calling Him out in the wilderness of the sinful world.

God let Jesus know that He was not alone even when Jesus felt all alone on the cross.

The devil cut the throat of Jesus' life and let it bleed out on the cross, but God had predestined His supernatural power to heal Jesus' wounds and raise Him from the dead with victory over the hungry, devouring wolf of death.

Greatness is the Lamb of God.

Glory and honor and praise to the Lamb of God, who is worthy to exist forever beyond all existence seen and unseen.

Worthy is the Lamb of God, who is Jesus Christ, to take away our sins and cast them into the deep sea.

Worthy is the Lamb of God, who is Jesus Christ, to carry all the world's governments on his shoulders.

Worthy is the Lamb of God, who is Jesus Christ, who is coming back again on the clouds of glory with all the angels to gather you and me and all of His children to take them to heaven.

Worthy is the Lamb of God, who is Jesus Christ, who has all power and glory in heaven and in other worlds.

Worthy is the Lamb of God, who is Jesus Christ, who stooped down very low to be slaughtered like a little helpless lamb to save you and me from our sins.

Every time that we sin against Jesus, we slaughter him over and over again.

A Heavenly and Universal Subject

The heart of earthly human beings is a subject in heaven for the angels to talk about amongst themselves.

The heart of earthly human beings is a very intense subject to the angels in heaven who talk to Jesus the most about man's heart rebelling against God.

Jesus talks to the angels to let them know that He has faithful people like Abel, Abraham, Jacob, Joseph, Moses, Job, Rahab, Esther, Jeremiah, King David, John the Baptist and like Mary Magdalene.

The heart of earthly human beings is a big subject in other worlds where there is no sin.

The perfect creatures in other worlds talk about the heart of earthly human beings to one another as they gather together to talk to Jesus about sinful men and women on earth.

Jesus tells them that He has faithful people like Noah, Joshua, Elijah, Hosea, Malachi, Peter, Stephen, Apostle Paul, Sarah, Jochebed, Rebekah, Ruth, Rachel, Zipporah, Hannah, Deborah, and many like Dorcas.

A heavenly and universal subject is about the heart of earthly human beings, who Jesus came into this world to save from our sins, not to condemn us earthly human beings in our sins.

The heart of earthly human beings is a heavenly and universal eternal subject for the holy angels and creatures in other worlds to talk about to you and me when Jesus Christ comes back again to take us to heaven where we will tell them that we gave our hearts to Jesus, who will defend our hearts throughout eternity in the presence of the angels and creatures in another worlds.

Jesus tells the angels and the creatures in another worlds that He has the power to not condemn the hearts of earthly human beings who He has redeemed back to God through His blood that was shed on the cross when He died and rose from the grave and this causes the angels and creatures in other worlds to rejoice in their hearts.

God is a Master Genius

God is a master genius who told Noah to build an ark to save him and his family and many animals from the flood.

God is a master genius who told Abraham to leave his native country and go to the Canaan land where his descendants would inherit the land.

God is a master genius who told Lot and his family to leave Solomon and Gomorrah before He destroy it with fire and brimstone.

God is a master genius who told Moses from the burning bush to go back to Egypt and tell his people that he will set them free.

God is a master genius who told Joshua to march his army around the Jericho walls once a day for six days and seven times on the seventh day so the walls would tumble down.

God told Elijah to meet with the false prophets of Baal at Mount Carmel to have a showdown about who is the true living God, who truly being the God of Elijah, burned up all the water in the trench around the altar.

God is a master genius who told a whale to swallow Jonah and keep him in his belly for three days because Jonah had disobeyed God and refused to go to Nineveh to tell the people to repent unto God.

God is a master genius who told Samuel to choose the shepherd boy David to fight the Philistine giant Goliath.

God is a master genius who told his son Jesus to come to this sinful world to save you and me from our sins.

No angel and no human being can be more genius than God.

Cross Over the Border of Heaven

One day, we will cross over the border of heaven and become citizens of heaven.

Heaven won't have a border patrol agent to keep you and me from crossing over the border into heaven.

There will be no spiritual illegal immigrant crossing over the border into heaven.

Only the righteous will have legal rights to cross over the border into heaven one day when Jesus Christ comes back again with our spiritual legal papers signed by Him for us to cross over the border of heaven.

There won't be any border walls to keep the righteous from crossing over.

There will be a border wall for the wicked who are spiritually illegal immigrants to Jesus.

Jesus will make you and me citizens of heaven, and there will be no prejudice, no discrimination and no injustice in the holy land of heaven.

No righteous man, woman, boy or girl will be mistreated in heaven, and there will be no spiritual illegal immigrants who could smuggle any drugs of sin into heaven.

You and I and all of God's righteous children will migrate to heaven one day to live in a heavenly mansion that Jesus built for us.

Every righteous man, woman, boy and girl is a spiritual illegal immigrant to the devil because this old sinful world is his home.

The devil loves to especially mistreat you and me with his temptations because he knows that we will one day be citizens of heaven.

We Can Only Believe

We can only believe that the Bible is real truth about the people in the Bible.

We can only believe that the things that happened in the Bible are real truth.

We can only believe that the holy angels are real.

We can only believe that the devil is real.

We can only believe that God is real.

We can only believe that Jesus Christ is real.

We can only believe that heaven is real.

We can only believe that hell is real.

The Bible says that God created the animals and we see them being real.

The Bible says that God created the creatures in the waters and we can see them being real.

The Bible says that God created the sun, moon and stars and we can see that those are real.

The Bible says that God created man and woman and we can see we are real.

We believe that we are real and we can see that we are real.

We can only believe that the Bible is real truth about all those people in the Bible.

We can only believe that the Bible is real truth about God, even though we have never seen Him.

The Bible says a lot of things that we can see to be real truth today.

The Bible talks about righteous people that we can see in this world today.

The Bible talks about wicked people that we can see in this world today.

The Bible talks about troubled times and we can see that in this world today.

The Bible talks about wars and we can see that in this world today.

The Bible talks about diseases and we can see that in this world today.

The Bible talks about people who we can see in this world today.

We can believe anything when we can truly believe the Bible that talks about life and death that we can see in this world today.

If we truly believe the Bible is truth, we cannot doubt that God the father, God the Son and God the Holy Spirit is real.

We can only believe in Jesus Christ, who we have never seen, but Jesus will save us from our sins if we believe in Him.

Jesus is the foundation for the Bible truth to stand on forever and ever.

Can't be too Spiritually High Up

You and I can't be too spiritually high up to not come down and meet people at their spiritual low.

We must come down from our spiritual high and help people to understand the bad things they are going through in their lives.

You and I can be on a holy high, but we must come down to meet hurting people on their spiritual level.

You and I can be on a righteous high, but we must come down to meet broken people on their spiritual level and let them know that Jesus can fix their hearts so they can love again.

You and I can be on a faithful high to move mountains, but we must come down to meet spiritually weak people on their level to encourage them to put their faith in Jesus, who can do anything but failed us.

You and I can't be too spiritually high up to not come down to meet people where they are in their sinful words when we can speak good inspiring words about the Lord to them to make them have a change of heart.

You and I can't be too spiritually high up to not come down to meet people where they are in their sinful deeds, when we can do the Lord's will in their presence for them to see us living right by God.

You and I can be on a Holy Ghost high, but we must come down to meet people on their level of being high on living by eyesight and let them know that unseen things are eternal in Jesus, who is all of the heavens and other worlds' rightful eternal heir who lives forever beyond this seen, temporary world.

The Only Way
That I can be a Christian

The only way that I can be a Christian is to be like you, my Lord and Savior Jesus Christ.

Being a Christian is being like you, O Lord.

I don't want to be a mean Christian.

I don't want to be a proud Christian.

I don't want to be a show-off Christian.

The only way that I can be a Christian is to be like you, my Lord and Savior Jesus Christ.

I don't want to be a high-minded Christian.

I don't want to be a sad Christian.

I don't want to be a gossiping Christian.

I don't want to be a gluttonous Christian.

I don't want to be in a discontent Christian.

I don't want to be a greedy Christian.

The only way that I can be a Christian is to be like you, my Lord and Savior Jesus Christ.

I don't want to be a lying Christian.

I don't want to be an unforgiving Christian.

I don't want to be a revengeful Christian.

I don't want to be a troublemaker Christian.

The only way that I can be a Christian is to be like you, my Lord and Savior Jesus Christ.

I don't want to be a hypocrite Christian.

I don't want to be a favoritism Christian.

I don't want to be a manipulating Christian.

I don't want to be a deceptive Christian.

I don't want to be an unbalanced Christian.

I don't want to be an unstable Christian.

I don't want to be an ignorant Christian.

The only way that I can be a Christian is to be like you, my Lord and Savior Jesus Christ.

I don't want to be a lawbreaker Christian.

I don't want to be a judgmental Christian.

I don't want to be a careless Christian.

I don't want to be an impolite Christian.

I don't want to be a selfish Christian.

I don't want to be a discouraging Christian.

Many people go to church and believe that they are Christians, but instead they're being like the devil in the presence of many people who believe that a Christian can talk any kind of way and act any kind of way and still be called a Christian.

The only way to be a Christian is to be like you, my Lord and Savior Jesus Christ, who lived on earth without sin to be the right example for a Christian to be like every day.

The Truth of God's Holy Word is All-Powerful

The truth of God's holy word is all-powerful.

The devil has no power over the truth.

The devil can't erase the truth.

The devil can't destroy the truth.

The devil can't enslave the truth.

The devil can't deceive the truth.

The devil can't kill the truth.

The devil can't trick the truth.

The devil can't brainwash the truth.

The truth is all-powerful and can set us free from the devil's lies.

The truth is all-powerful and can make a liar look bad.

The truth is all-powerful and can make the guilty verdict in the verdict in the courtroom.

The truth is all-powerful and can change anyone's mind to believe the truth.

The truth is all-powerful and can make the innocent look good.

The truth is all-powerful and can make false accusers look like they are confused.

The truth is all-powerful and can draw out the deepest secrets.

The truth is all-powerful and can shine through the darkest soul.

The truth is all-powerful and can cheer a sad soul.

The truth is all-powerful and can heal a broken spirit.

The truth is all-powerful and can make an enemy into a friend.

The truth of God's holy word is all powerful above and beyond the devil's lies and schemes.

The truth of God's holy word is all powerful and can change a delusional mind so that it thinks on what is real and surely the truth.

The truth of God's holy word is all-powerful and eternal above and beyond all kinds of lies that are temporary and will burn in hellfire and brimstone when the Lord destroys this sinful world one day.

The truth of God's holy word is all-powerful and only foolish people will try to compromise the truth of God's holy word that will never change for anyone in this world.

The Devil Tried to Tempt Jesus

The devil tried to tempt Jesus with false worship.

The devil wanted Jesus to worship him.

The devil tried to tempt Jesus with pride.

The devil tried to tempt Jesus to steal.

The devil tried to tempt Jesus to kill.

The devil tried to tempt Jesus with adultery.

The devil tried to tempt Jesus with fornication.

The devil tried to tempt Jesus with jealousy.

The devil tried to tempt Jesus with homosexuality.

The devil tried to tempt Jesus with gluttony.

The devil tried to tempt Jesus to lust.

The devil tried to tempt Jesus with violence.

The devil tried to tempt Jesus to lie.

The devil tried to tempt Jesus to disobey His parents.

The devil tried to tempt Jesus with intemperance.

The devil tried to tempt Jesus with impatience.

The Devil tried to tempt Jesus with covetousness.

The devil tried to tempt Jesus with wealth.

The devil tried to tempt Jesus with self-ambition.

The devil could not tempt Jesus to sin against God.

The devil failed in all of his attempts because Jesus stayed in prayer and always spoke the holy word of God to the devil and his human agents.

Jesus was always obedient to God, even when He humbled himself onto His death on the cross.

The devil tried to tempt Jesus to gossip.

The devil tried to tempt Jesus with fear.

The devil tried to tempt Jesus to hold grudges.

The devil tried to tempt Jesus with deception.

The devil tried to tempt Jesus with greed.

The devil tried to tempt Jesus with delusion.

The devil tried to tempt Jesus with every temptation he could think of, but he failed in all of his attempts.

Jesus was tempted by the devil in many ways that you and I will not be tempted because of Jesus' victory over all of the devil's temptations.

Jesus' victory over the devil's temptations has put a limit on the devil and made him not able to tempt you and me with more than what we can bear.

The devil tried to tempt Jesus with the full force of his temptations, but Jesus was filled with the Holy Ghost who gave Him the power to resist all of the devil's temptations out in the wilderness where Jesus was tempted for 40 days and 40 nights before He began His ministry to save sinners from being lost in their sins.

The Israel of Today

The Israel of today is supposed to set the right example before all the other nations in this world.

The Israel of today is supposed to love God and keep His Commandments that the Bible talks about.

The Bible talks a lot about Israel being God's chosen nation of people to worship the only one true living God before all the world.

The Bible talks a lot about Israel worshiping idol gods.

The Bible talks a lot about Israel winning wars.

The Bible talks a lot about Israel rebelling against God.

The Israel of today is still God's chosen nation to spread the gospel of Jesus Christ to all the world.

No other nation is God's chosen nation to lead souls to be saved in Jesus.

The Israel of today is not in the limelight of this world like the old Israel that was more repentant unto God.

The Israel nation of today has its faithful and obedient children unto the Lord Jesus Christ.

They are not in the limelight of this world with their faith and obedience unto the Lord.

There are other nations that love to put on a show with their religion of self-ambition to gain popularity.

The Israel of today is on the move to win souls to Jesus, who has his spiritual Israelites like you and me who love and obey Jesus.

The Israel of today has its rebellious people, but God is still in control of Israel today and will bless His few chosen ones like He blessed Jacob and named him Israel.

Only One Body Language

There are many languages spoken all around the world, but there is only one body language spoken every day.

The body language is the only language that everyone can pretty much understand clearly.

Body language can be as clear as a crystal-clear glass.

We can hear what people say in other languages but may not know what they say, but we can read their body language and know what they do.

A smile is a body language that people all around the world can understand.

A helping hand is a body language that people all around the world can understand.

Shedding some tears is a body language that people all around the world can understand.

Eating food is a body language that people all around the world can understand.

Lying down to sleep is a body language that people all around the world can understand.

Coughing is a body language that people all around the world can understand.

People all around the world can pretty much figure out what body language is saying, when speaking different languages in words can be confusing because of not knowing what is said in a different language.

Being very angry is a body language that people all around the world can understand.

Fighting is a body language that people all around the world can understand.

Kissing is a body language that people all around the world can understand.

Holding hands as a body language that people all around the world can understand.

Laughing is a body language that people all around the world can understand.

Hugging is a body language that people all around the world can understand.

God had created the many languages for people to speak in words, but God has also given us all one body language so we can pretty much understand the nonverbal body language all around the world.

There are people who can speak different languages, but body language pretty much needs no interpreter

All around the world if we're drinking some water it is a body language that everyone can understand.

God gave us all one body language to understand, when words can be misunderstood even in the same language.

The Lord Can Use Nature

The Lord can use nature to clear our minds from worry.

The Lord can use nature to clear our minds from confusion.

The Lord can use nature to clear our minds from anger.

The Lord can use nature to clear our minds from believing lies.

The Lord can use nature to clear our minds from greed.

The Lord can use nature to clear our minds from pride.

The Lord can use nature to clear our minds from self-ambition.

The Lord can use nature to clear our minds from being impatient.

The Lord can use nature to clear our minds from discouragement.

The Lord can use nature to clear our minds from disappointments.

The Lord can use nature to clear our minds from doubt about what He can do for us.

The Lord can use nature to clear our minds to think on Him.

The Lord can use nature to clear our minds for us to see His love for us.

The Lord can use nature to clear our minds for us to think on His goodness.

The Lord can use nature to clear our minds for us to think on His mercy unto us.

The Lord can use nature to clear our minds for us to think on His amazing grace that He has given to us.

The Lord can use nature to clear our minds for us to think on His patience for us.

Nature is an open bible that we can study about the Lord who is also in nature every day.

The Lord can use nature to clear our minds from the hustle and bustle in this temporary world.

The Lord can use nature to clear our minds from the troubles in this world and give us peace of mind as if trouble didn't exist at all.

The Lord can use nature to clear our minds from things that are not true.

The Lord can use nature to clear our minds from thinking about our pain.

The Lord can use nature to clear our minds for us to think on loving Him and keeping His Commandments.

God Speaks His Love for Us Through Nature

God speaks His love for us through the trees that stand tall in God's love.

God speaks His love for us through the grass that covers the ground in God's love.

God speaks His love for us through the leaves that fall on the ground in God's love.

God speaks His love for us through the mountains that have high cliffs in God's love.

God speaks His love for us through the valleys that are low down in God's love.

God speaks His love for us through the hills that are high and low in God's love.

God speaks His love for us through the rivers that flow in God's love.

God speaks His love for us through the oceans that are deep in God's love.

God speaks His love for us through the sky that hovers over this world in God's love.

God speaks His love for us through the sunlight that shines God's love.

God speaks His love for us through the moonlight that glows God's love.

God speaks His love through the stars the sparkle God's love.

God speaks His love for us through the flowers that beautify God's love.

God speaks His love for us through nature every day that nature is a visible Bible for us to see God's love in nature where God also speaks His truth to us.

It's a Good Thing

It's a good thing to get people's opinions if they mean you good and well to help you better yourself in what you do.

Everyone's opinions are not good and can do you and me bad.

You and I don't know it all, for even a child can give us his or her opinion to do us some good.

It's a good thing to get people's honest opinions, because there are people who can see what you and I don't see.

Someone's opinion will be bad if he or she is not honest with you and me.

It's a good thing to get more than one opinion because people are different.

Just because people are different doesn't mean that she is right and he is wrong with their opinions.

The best opinions that you and I can get are from the people we know and believe to be honest with us.

Jesus' opinions were always honest in His holy word.

Jesus spoke His opinion to a rich young ruler, telling him to give up all that he had and follow Him.

Jesus' opinion was truthful to the rich young ruler who tried to duck and dodge away from Jesus' opinion of him that was true.

One of Jesus' disciples named Thomas had one opinion about Jesus until Jesus let him touch His wounds and then Thomas realized that Jesus was real flesh and bone in his eyesight.

It's a good thing to get people's honest opinions and it is a good learning process to help you and me see that we need to not be self-centered as if we know at all.

O Lord, You Always Know

O Lord, you always know how to deal with people who cheat other people.

O Lord, you always know how to deal with people who lie to other people.

O Lord, you always know how to deal with people who lie about other people.

O Lord, you always know how to deal with people who kill other people.

O Lord, you always know how to deal with people who rob other people.

O Lord, you always know how to deal with people who gossip about other people.

O Lord, you always know how to deal with people who deceive other people.

O Lord, you always know how to deal with people who talk bad about other people.

O Lord, you always know how to deal with people who treat other people bad.

O Lord, you always know how to deal with people who are rude to other people.

O Lord, you always know how to deal with people who are jealous of other people.

O Lord, you always know how to deal with people who are envious of other people.

O Lord, you always know how to deal with people who hate other people.

O Lord, you always know how to deal with people who disrespect other people.

O Lord, you always know how to deal with people who ignore other people.

O Lord, you always know how to deal with people who won't help other people.

O Lord, you always know how to deal with people who won't pay other people what they owe them.

O Lord, you always know how to deal with people who aren't faithful to their spouses.

O Lord, you always know how to deal with people who neglect their children.

O Lord, you always know how to deal with people who throw indirect words at other people.

O Lord, you always know how to deal with people who manipulate other people.

O Lord, you always know how to deal with people who put other people down.

O Lord, you always know how to deal with people who are proud.

O Lord, you always know how to deal with people who turn their backs on you.

O Lord, you always know how to deal with people who treat other people unfairly.

O Lord, you always know how to deal with people who are violent to other people.

O Lord, you always know how to deal with people who use other people.

O Lord, you always know how to deal with people who don't forgive other people.

O Lord, you always know how to deal with people who hurt other people.

O Lord, you always know how to deal with people who are hypocrites.

O Lord, you always know how to deal with people of the world.

O Lord, you always know how to deal with people who are selfish.

O Lord, you always know how to deal with people who are greedy for worldly gain.

O Lord, you will always know how to deal with people who act like they are better than other people.

O Lord, you always know how to deal with people who abuse animals.

O Lord, you always know how to deal with people who don't love You and don't keep Your Commandments.

O Lord, you always know how to deal with people to help them to see the truth.

O Lord, you always know how to deal with people to save their souls.

People Can Crowd up Together

People can crowd up together at a wedding.

People can crowd up together at a funeral.

People can crowd up together at an amusement park.

People can crowd up together at a basketball game.

If people crowd up together at church, then Jesus Christ would have come back on the clouds of glory a long time ago.

People can crowd up at a football game.

People can crowd up at a baseball game.

People can crowd up at a golf tournament.

People can crowd up at a tennis match.

People can crowd up at the Olympics.

If people crowd up at the church, this world would be a much better place to live in.

People can crowd up at a car race track.

People can crowd up at the Oscar awards.

People can crowd up at the Emmy awards.

People can crowd up at the movie theaters.

People can crowd up at a concert.

People can crowd up at a party.

People can crowd up at a rodeo show.

People can crowd up at a modeling show.

If people crowd up at every church, then there would be a lot less crimes in this world.

People can crowd up at a riot.

People can crowd up at a food bank.

People can crowd up at a store.

People can crowd up at a family reunion.

People can crowd up at a horse race.

People can crowd up at a dog show.

If people crowd up at the church, then God would spare this world from a lot of distress.

People can crowd up at a restaurant.

People can crowd up at an event.

People can crowd up at a boxing match.

People can crowd up at a martial arts match.

People can crowd up at a shopping mall.

People can crowd up at a talk show.

People can crowd up at a courthouse.

If people crowd up at the church, then the hypocrites in the church will truly know that their time is up for Jesus to cast them out of his church.

If people crowd up together at every church, then Jesus will bring them all into His true church having every wheat being filled by the Holy Spirit of God.

Dreams in the Night

Dreams in the night can come from what we do.

Dreams in the night can come from what we see.

Dreams in the night can come from what we hear.

Dreams in the night can come from what we go through in our lives.

There are some dreams in the night that we just won't understand when we wake up out of those dreams.

Dreams in the night can come from our activities in the day.

Dreams in the night can come from stress.

Dreams in the night can come from bad experiences.

A dream in the night can come from the Lord.

When we dream in our sleep it can be like living in another world.

When we dream in our sleep it can be like being in an eternal place.

Some of our dreams in the night make us just want to stay there in our dreams and never leave.

We remember some of our dreams in the night and we forget some of our dreams in the night.

The Lord won't put on us more than what we can bear, even though in our dreams in the night we travel into the unknown places of dreams.

Every dream in our sleep in the night has a meaning that only the Lord knows and can tell us what our dreams mean.

The Lord knows that we don't need to know what every dream means in our sleep in the night.

If we knew what every dream meant, we wouldn't be able to handle it, especially the bad dreams in the night.

The Lord is even merciful to us in our dreams in the night.

It's the Lord who changes the scenes in our dreams and takes us to different places in our dreams for His purpose.

We must pray that the Lord won't allow the devil to give us a dream in the night because the devil gives nightmares that causes some people to die in their sleep.

Dreams from the devil come from not yielding to the voice of the Holy Spirit and living a wicked life.

Dreams from the Lord in the night will surely cause you and me to wake up refreshed in the early morning to seek out the Lord and pray to the Lord for His guidance in our life for another day.

Trials

You and I must go through some trials for Jesus' holy name sake.

We can read the Bible and know what Jesus went through for us all to be here today.

Some trials that we go through may last for years and years, but the Lord knows what it will take for Him to mold and shape you and me to be like He wants us to be to glorify His holy name.

Going through trials for Jesus' holy name sake will surely be a testimony to our brothers and sisters in the Lord.

They will know that it's the Lord keeping you and me mentally, emotionally and spiritually strong in our trials.

In our trials, the Lord will mold and shape us to be His church bride, ready to go back with Him to heaven one day when He comes back again to take us there for being saved in Him.

Going through trials for Jesus' holy name sake is to make us be on fire in spreading the gospel of Jesus Christ.

Going through trials for Jesus' holy name sake is to make us keep our eyes on Jesus and not on those who are living by eyesight and have no faith in Jesus.

Going through trials for Jesus' holy name sake is not to break us down in seeing things not getting better, because Jesus will repair our lives through our trials that will only break down those who don't put their trust in Jesus through their trials.

You and I must go through some trials for Jesus' holy name sake if we love Him who knew all of our trials before we were born to not do and not know anything.

We are going through nothing much at all compared to what Jesus went through, so you and I should have no excuses to not love and obey Him who got the victory over all of our trials.

You and I can give all of our trials to Jesus, who will make us feel as light as a feather floating in the air if we trust Him to bring us through our trials.

Cannot Be Too

Our hearts cannot be too broken for the Lord to fix to love again.

Our pain cannot be too much for the Lord to soothe.

Our disappointments cannot be too disappointing for the Lord to make good.

Our time cannot be too off for the Lord to be on time.

Our grief cannot be too sad for the Lord to give us joy.

Our bad days cannot be too bad for the Lord to make a good day.

Our troubled times cannot be too troublesome for the Lord to ease.

Our money cannot be too low for the Lord to stretch out.

Our minds cannot be too worldly for the Lord to give us thoughts on spiritual things.

Our eyes cannot be too blind in darkness for the Lord to open them so we can see His love.

Our minds cannot be too confused for the Lord to understand and make clear.

Our thoughts cannot be too deep for the Lord to bring out in words.

Our bad habits cannot be too bad for the Lord to make good.

Our mistakes cannot be too much for the Lord to help us to stop making the same mistakes again.

Our life cannot be too messed up for the Lord to straighten it out.

Our life cannot be too lost in sin for the Lord to save us.

The Way that We Dress

The way that we dress has a lot to do with who we are.

If we dress with modest apparel then we are not looking to draw attention to ourselves.

The way that we dress can tell people something good about us.

The way that we dress can tell people something bad about us.

The way that we dress can draw some bad attention.

The way that we dress can draw some good attention.

There are people who are very aware of how they dress.

There are people who are not so aware of how they dress.

There are people who will dress up to draw attention to themselves.

The way that we dress can cause people to have good feelings about us.

The way that we dress can cause people to have bad feelings about us.

We Christian folks are supposed to dress in modest apparel every day, and we should dress for people to see Jesus in us.

The way that we dress has a lot to do with how we feel about ourselves.

There are people who feel bad and will try to hide it by dressing up with expensive clothes.

There are people who feel bad and will try to hide it by dressing in a seductive way.

There are people who feel good and will wear plain looking clothes.

The way that we dress can prolong our lives.

The way that we dress can shorten our lives.

The way that we dress will please the Lord or displease the Lord.

The way that we dress can surely rub off on little children who want to dress like us.

The Traffic of Life

The traffic of life can get heavy with cars of discouragement.

The traffic of life can get heavy with pick-up trucks of strife.

The traffic of life can get heavy with SUVs of disappointments.

The traffic of life can get heavy with minivans of covetousness.

The traffic of life can get heavy with buses of brokenness.

The traffic of life can get heavy with motorcycles of impatience.

The traffic of life can get heavy with tractor trailer trucks of greed.

The traffic of life can get heavy with RVs of immortality.

The traffic of life can get heavy with dump trucks of dumping out lies.

The traffic of life can get heavy with accidents of grief.

The traffic of life can jam up our minds with worry if we don't keep our minds on Jesus.

The traffic of life can jam up our eyes with living by eyesight if we don't live by faith in Jesus.

The traffic of life can jam up our hearts with grudges if we don't forgive those who wrong us like Jesus will forgive them if they confess and repent of their sins unto Him.

Only Jesus can clear up the traffic jam in our lives so that no vehicles of the devil can jam up our walk with Jesus on the strait and narrow pathway.

Those Who are Closest to You

Those who are closest to you can let you down if they don't love Jesus.

Those who are closest to you can disappoint you if they don't love Jesus.

Those who are closest to you can hurt you if they don't love Jesus.

Those who are closest to you can turn their backs on you if they don't love Jesus.

Those who are closest to you can be your enemy if they don't love Jesus.

Those who are closest to you can deceive you if they don't love Jesus.

Those who are closest to you can confuse you if they don't love Jesus.

Those who are closest to you can hold grudges against you if they don't love Jesus.

Those who are closest to you can turn against you if they don't love Jesus.

Jesus' disciples were the closest ones to him, but Judas betrayed Jesus for 30 pieces of silver and with a kiss.

Peter denied Jesus three times for the cock to crow.

Those who are closest to you can fail you.

If you let Jesus be the closest one to you, Jesus will never hurt you.

If you let Jesus be the closest one to you, Jesus will never let you down.

If you let Jesus be the closest one to you, Jesus will never disappoint you.

If you let Jesus be the closest one to you, Jesus will never turn his back on you.

If you let Jesus be the closest one to you, Jesus will never deceive you.

If you let Jesus be the one closest to you, Jesus will never fool you.

If you let Jesus be the closest one to you, Jesus will never fail you.

If you let Jesus be the closest one to you, Jesus will never leave you or forsake you.

If you let Jesus be the closest one to you, Jesus will never discourage you.

You Can't Help Everybody

You can't help every sick person.

You can't help every disabled person.

You can't help every homeless person.

You can't help every poor person.

You can't help every suicidal person.

You can't help every mentally ill person.

You can't help every ignorant person.

You can't help every brokenhearted person.

You can't help every sad person.

You can't help every grieving person.

You can't help every discouraged person.

You can't be everywhere to help everybody.

Only God is everywhere to help everybody.

If you try to help everybody, you will get weary.

If you try to help everybody, you would run out of money.

If you try to help everybody, you would get very exhausted.

You can't help every dying person.

You can't help every widow.

You can't help every orphan.

No Christian can help every wicked person to confess and repent of their sins and turn to God who is everywhere at the same time to help everybody great and small.

If there is one person who you just can't help and that person might be in your family, don't beat yourself up if you can't help that person who may not want your help.

Only God can help everybody everywhere at the same time because only God is everywhere when you and I can only be in one place at a time and may fail to help a brother or sister in the church.

No matter how much you love to help people, you can help the wrong person who won't appreciate your help, but God can open up that person's eyes to see how wrong they are for refusing your help.

Doubt

The devil loves to put doubt in our minds so that we don't believe what the Lord can do for us.

To doubt the Lord is like drinking poison.

To doubt the Lord is like walking in front of a speeding tractor trailer truck.

To doubt the Lord is like drowning in the deepest ocean.

To doubt the Lord is like getting burned up in fire.

To doubt the Lord is like jumping out of a plane without a parachute.

To doubt the Lord is like committing suicide.

To doubt the Lord is like falling off a mountain cliff.

To doubt the Lord is like being paralyzed.

To doubt the Lord is like losing your mind.

To doubt the Lord is like hanging yourself.

The devil has his human agents who love to put doubt in our minds about what the Lord can do for us.

To doubt the Lord is like living in a dark cave.

To doubt the Lord is like cutting out your own tongue.

To doubt the Lord is like breaking your own leg.

To doubt the Lord is the worst kind of failure in anyone's life.

Even if we doubt the Lord, he can work things out in our lives, because the Lord is merciful toward us and will not let our doubt get the victory over our lives.

The Lord is merciful to overpower our doubt about Him who can set us free.

Before It's Too Late

It doesn't matter to the Lord what people have done.

The Lord wants people to confess and repent of their sins and live for Him before it's too late.

The Lord doesn't take any pleasure in seeing people lost in their sins.

The Lord wants to save as many people as He can from being lost.

Today is the time for all the living to live right unto the Lord before it's too late.

Any day the Lord could close His probation on this world and stand up and say that it is finished.

The Lord doesn't want anyone to be lost in their sins, but we all have a free will to choose to love and obey the Lord or choose to love and obey the devil.

The Lord will take no pleasure in destroying the devil and his fallen angels and his human agents in hell fire and brimstone one day.

The Lord will take no pleasure in destroying what He created to give Him their worship.

Living in the darkness of sin affects the Lord in nothing but bad ways every day.

So many so-called Christians are spiritually numb and feel no bad affects from living in sin.

The Lord doesn't want even those so-called Christians to be lost in their sins when one day it will be too late for many people to be saved in the Lord Jesus Christ.

The Lord is all about saving lost souls because all souls belong to the Lord and every soul will answer to Him on judgment day.

Being too late means that there is no more chance to repent unto the Lord, who we must repent of our sins while we live.

We just don't know whether today might be our last day in the land of the living.

It will be too late to confess and repent of our sins unto the Lord when we are in the grave.

God Will Not Change the Truth

God will not change the truth of His holy word for anyone.

God will show His mercy on us but the truth of His holy word will set us free from the devil's lies.

God is merciful, but God will not change the truth of His holy word that is for us today, tomorrow and forever.

We must not take God's mercy for granted as if we can sin against Him and make excuses before Him to change His holy word to fit in with our own will.

God's holy will is the truth of His holy word that mercy can't change because God will judge us by His truth, and His mercy will not override this.

God will not change the truth to please anyone.

God's mercy will run out when God closes His grace on this world, but God's truth will be around forever and will never change.

If we fully continue to reject the truth of God's holy word, God will not extend His mercy towards us.

God's truth is alive and can prolong our lives, but many people will use God's mercy as an excuse to do what they want to do.

God says that His truth will set us free.

God didn't say that His mercy will set us free.

We can thank God for His mercy, which we should never take for granted as if God would excuse us from doing wrong things when we know what is right to do.

God will not change the truth of His holy word which will stand forever, while God's mercy will run out one day for Jesus to stand up and say that it is finished.

O Lord, You are a Great God

O Lord, You keep me in my right mind, and that is great.

O Lord, You give me strength from day to day, and that is great.

O Lord, You answer my prayers, and that is great.

O Lord You are a great God every day.

O Lord, You wake me up in the morning, and that is great.

O Lord You protect me from harm and danger, and that is great.

O Lord, You are a great God every day.

O Lord, You have blessed me financially, and that is great.

O Lord, You have blessed me with my physical health, and that is great.

O Lord, You blessed me with food to eat, and that is great.

O Lord, You are a great God.

O Lord, You give me peace of mind, and that is great.

O Lord, You show mercy on me, and that is great.

O Lord, You love me, and that is great.

O Lord, You forgive me of my sins, and that is great.

O Lord, You cleanse me of my sins, and that is great.

O Lord, You give me spiritual gifts, and that is great.

O Lord, You are a great God.

O Lord, You spare my life for me to see this day, and that is great.

O Lord, You supply all of my needs, and that is great.

O Lord, You are a great God to me every day.

O Lord, You help me to be content, and that is great.

O Lord, You are worthy to be a great God.

O Lord, You are worthy to be a great God in heaven and on earth.

No one can ever be greater than You.

O Lord, You lift me up in this uncertain world.

O Lord, You pick me up with the truth of Your holy word when the devil's lies try to knock me down.

O Lord, You are worthy to be a great God.

O Lord, You are a great God above and beyond all the angels in heaven.

As I Get Older

As I get older, my life gets better for loving and obeying my Lord and Savior Jesus Christ.

As I get older, my life gets better for trusting Jesus to give me the victory through my trials.

As I get older, my life gets better as I pray to Jesus without ceasing.

As I get older, my life gets better for speaking the Bible truth to people with love.

As I get older, my life gets better for trying my best to eat healthy food because my body belongs to the Lord.

As I get older, my life gets better for making a lot of good choices to please the Lord.

As I get older, my life gets better for not staying up late at night.

As I get older, my life gets better for reading my Bible every day.

As I get older, my life gets better as my faith grows stronger in the Lord.

As I get older, my life gets better for getting a good night's sleep.

As I get older, my life gets better because of my Lord and Savior Jesus Christ who blesses my life.

As I get older, my life gets better for living right unto the Lord.

As I get older, my life gets better because the Lord supplies all of my needs.

As I get older, my life gets better for keeping my eyes on Jesus.

As I get older, my life gets better for returning a faithful tithes and offerings unto Jesus.

As I get older, my life gets better for getting more spiritually mature in Jesus.

As I get older, my life gets better for getting wiser in doing the Lord's will.

As I get older, my life gets better for denying self and picking up my cross to follow Jesus.

As I get older, my life gets better for giving testimonies about what Jesus brought me through.

As I get older, my life gets better for being a witness of Jesus.

As I get older, my life gets better for being like Jesus.

As I get older, my life gets better because Jesus gives me the strength to get through the day.

As I get older, my life gets better for using my spiritual gift to edify the church of Jesus Christ.

As I get older, my life gets better for confessing and repenting of my sins unto Jesus Christ.

To Live Right By Example

You don't have to be a pastor of a church to live right by example.

You don't have to be a church leader to live right by example.

You can be a regular church member and live right by example unto the Lord.

You and I know we are supposed to live right unto the Lord.

If the pastor is not living right by example, you can live right by example.

If any church leader is not living right by example, you can live right by example unto the Lord.

Living right by example is for everyone who claims to be a Christian.

To be like Jesus Christ is living right by what He says in His holy word.

If some people in your church are doing wrong, you can live right by example in their eyes to help them to be wiser and repent unto the Lord.

You can live right by example unto the Lord, even if some people in the church just don't want to stand firm on God's holy word.

There are some church folks who would rather please men then please the Lord.

They take part in doing the doctrines of men instead of living right by the word of God.

To live right by example can be a lonely road to walk down because some church members will leave you and me all alone to live right by example while they are taking part in things that go against God's holy word.

To live right by example is to live right by God's holy word before the people of the world, so the Lord can bring many of them into the church because of you and me living right by example.

The Closer I Get to You, O Lord

The closer I get to You, O Lord, the more you show me how bad I am.

The closer I get to You, O Lord, the more you show me that I need to confess and repent of my sins unto you.

The closer that I get to You, O Lord, the more you show me how much I need You, Lord.

The closer I get to You, O Lord the more you show me that I need more faith in You, O Lord.

The closer I get to You, O Lord, the more you show me that you brought me this far in my life.

The closer I get to You, O Lord, the more you show me that I still have a long way to go to be like You, O Lord.

The closer I get to You, O Lord, the more You show me that I need to love You more than anyone and anything in this life.

The closer I get to You, O Lord, the more You show me that I need to trust You to work out everything for me.

The closer I get to You, O Lord, the more You show me that I need to love my brothers and sisters in the church.

The closer I get to You, O Lord, the more You show me that I need to keep Your Ten Commandments.

The closer I get to You, O Lord, the more You show me that I need to deny myself and pick up my cross and follow You.

The closer I get to You, O Lord, the more You show me that I am nothing without You.

The closer I get to You, O Lord, the more You show me that my good works can't save me because only You can save me from my sins.

The closer I get to You, my Lord and Savior Jesus Christ, the more You show me that I am a sinner saved through Your amazing grace.

We're Supposed To

We're supposed to eat healthy food.

We're supposed to drink clean water.

We're supposed to take a shower.

We're supposed to brush our teeth.

We're supposed to put on clothes.

We are supposed to put socks on our feet.

We're supposed to put on our shoes.

We're supposed to sleep in our beds.

We're supposed to sit down and rest.

We're supposed to work.

We're supposed to talk.

We're supposed to listen.

We're supposed to keep our weight down.

We're supposed to not overdo anything.

We're supposed to tell the truth.

We're supposed to comb our hair.

We're supposed to get an education.

We're supposed to park our cars.

We're supposed to drive safely.

We're supposed to have a roof over our heads.

We're supposed to take care of ourselves.

We're supposed to take care of our children.

We're supposed to take care of our pets.

We're supposed to treat people right.

We're supposed to have eyes to see.

We're supposed to have ears to hear.

We're supposed to have hands to hold.

We're supposed to have legs and feet to walk.

We're supposed to have a mouth to talk and eat food.

We're supposed to have a nose to breathe.

We're supposed to have a mind to think.

We're supposed to have a heart to feel.

We're supposed to survive.

Just because we're supposed to do something doesn't mean it's a command, but when God commands us to love Him and keep His Commandments, that is a command beyond what we're supposed to do.

A command from God is greater than something you're supposed to do.

A command from God is more rewarding than something you're supposed to do.

A command from God is more meaningful than something you're supposed to do.

A command from God is more real than something you're supposed to do.

A command from God is far more lasting than something you're supposed to do.

We're supposed to not make the same mistakes over and over again, but God's commandments are holy, righteous and perfect and have no mistakes because God cannot make mistakes.

A Thief, a Murderer and a Liar

The devil is a thief, a murderer and a liar every day.

The devil loves to steal every day.

The devil loves to kill every day.

The devil loves to tell lies every day.

The devil hates what God gives to us and the devil loves to steal it from us.

The devil would kill you and me on any day if God allows him to.

The devil loves for us to lie every day, but the devil also loves to tell us lies.

If the devil wasn't a thief, then why would God call him a thief?

If the devil wasn't a murderer, then why would God call him a murderer?

If the devil wasn't a liar, then why would God call him a liar?

The devil would have killed Job if God had allowed the devil to kill Job, whose wife had told him to curse God and die.

Jezebel was one of the devil's human agents who wanted to kill Elijah, the prophet of God.

The devil has always been a thief, a murderer and a liar from the beginning of his rebellion against God, who many people believed to be a thief, a murderer and a liar because that's what the devil tells many people who don't believe in God's son, Jesus Christ.

Can we ever imagine how it would be if God was all about stealing, killing and lying?

We all would be better off never being born if God was an evil God.

The Bible says that the devil is a thief, a murderer and a liar and if that's not true then the Bible would be a lie.

The devil doesn't want us to believe that he will steal from us.

The devil doesn't want us to believe that he will kill us.

The devil doesn't want us to believe that he will lie to us and lie on us.

The devil wants us to believe that God is a thief, a murderer and a liar.

The devil wants us to believe that God loves to take away life, when it's the devil who loves to take away life that God loves to give.

God is life and not death.

It's the devil who loves to use death to his advantage to kill even innocent men, women, boys and girls, as well as innocent animals.

If it was God who steals from everybody, or God who takes away everybody's life, or God who lies to everybody, then why does the Bible say that the devil is a thief, a murderer and a liar?

The Bible says that God is love.

It's the devil who wants you and me to die being lost in our sins.

If God was to let the devil have his way all the time, then the devil would cause every nation to shoot off nuclear missiles to kill everybody around the world.

God is all about giving life and not taking away life, which is what the devil will do if God allows him to.

If God allows the devil to have his way all the time and lets the devil put on us more than what we can bear, no one would be saved and we will die in our sins.

The devil is all about killing us so we will be lost in our sins because he doesn't want anyone to go to heaven and live forever.

There were times in the Bible that God put people to death, but there was always a good reason for God to do this.

The devil's reasons are always evil when he puts people to death, and he puts people to death whether they are good or evil.

The devil is a thief, a murderer and a liar and he will be that way until Jesus Christ comes back again to give eternal life to all who are saved in Him.

The devil put a lot of people and animals to death because he is a murderer.

When God puts people to death it is because He wants to save their souls.

When God puts people to death is because they are too wicked.

The devil doesn't care about putting anyone to death or whether they are rich or poor, educated or not educated.

The devil doesn't care about putting people to death or whether they good or bad, because the devil is a thief, a murderer and a liar who will steal, kill and lie just being who he is every day.

The devil doesn't care about who he steals from every day.

The devil doesn't care about who he lies to and lies on every day.

Good People

The devil has his human agents who love to kill good people who are young, middle-aged and old.

The devil has his human agents who love to kill good people in every neighborhood.

The devil has his human agents who love to kill good people on the highway and local roads.

The devil has his human agents who love to kill good people on their jobs.

The devil has his human agents who love to kill good people in college.

The devil has his human agents who love to kill good people whether they go to church or don't go to church.

The devil has his human agents who love to kill good people in the big cities.

The devil has his human agents who love to kill people in the small towns.

The devil has his human agents who love to kill good people no matter what the color of their skin.

The devil has his human agents who love to kill good people at parties.

The devil has his human agents who love to kill good people living in war zones.

The devil has his human agents who love to kill good people with guns.

The devil knows that good people belong to the Lord.

The devil knows that good people have a good chance to make it to heaven where he can't ever live again.

The devil knows that God smiles down on good people.

The devil knows that he can't use good people to go around looking to kill people.

The devil knows that especially good Christian people are the reason why God hasn't closed His probation on this world because He wants to give His good Christian people more time to win souls to be saved in His Son, Jesus Christ, before it's too late.

Spiritual Things

The people of the world don't think on spiritual things because their minds are on the seen material things.

The people of the world don't think on the unseen spiritual God who created the unseen things and seen things.

Every day, God is spiritual and is the highest spirit over His ministering spirits of angels in heaven.

The people of the world will only think of material things like money, houses, cars, trucks, airplanes, clothes, jewelry and many more material things that are temporary.

Even many church folks will think on material things day after day, even though the Bible is spiritual and connects you and me to God the Father, God the Son and God the Holy Spirit, who is spiritual forever and ever.

Spiritual things are eternal and will vitalize our souls, but material things are temporary and will wear us down and make us weary.

God is the highest spirit to fill our minds with spiritual things that will give us peace of mind and joy in our hearts to do God's holy will.

We true children of God are spiritually-minded people who are real and true about spreading the gospel of Jesus Christ to the people of the world.

Spiritual things are far from the minds of the people of the world, and even far from the minds of many church folks who live by the things that they see in this temporary world.

The unseen spiritual things are like the air that we breathe but can't see, the air that keeps us alive.

God is a spiritual God who we don't see, but we surely know to call on Him, especially if our life is in great danger.

Spiritual things are from God, as are material things that God is not against us having, but it's wrong to put material things above a spiritual God.

Keeping our minds on spiritual things is like having an open window for the fresh air of heaven to flow through our minds with God's love to mend our spirits that sin breaks into pieces if we don't love and obey Jesus Christ.

The Way that We Watch for Jesus

The way that we watch for Jesus coming back again is to have a relationship with Jesus.

The way that we watch for Jesus coming back again is to pray to Jesus without ceasing.

The way that we watch for Jesus coming back again is to spread the gospel of Jesus Christ.

The way that we watch for Jesus coming back again is to give testimonies about what Jesus brought us through.

The way that we watch for Jesus coming back again is to be a witness of Jesus.

The way that we watch for Jesus coming back again is to use our spiritual gifts to edify the church.

The way that we watch for Jesus coming back again is to tell the truth about Jesus in love.

The way that we watch for Jesus coming back again is to win souls to Jesus.

The way that we watch for Jesus coming back again is to love Jesus and keep His commandments.

The way that we watch for Jesus coming back again is to work out our own soul's salvation.

The way that we watch for Jesus coming back again is to deny self and pick up one's cross and follow Jesus.

The way that we watch for Jesus coming back again is to keep our faith and trust in Jesus.

The way that we watch for Jesus coming back again is to keep our hope in Jesus.

The way that we watch for Jesus coming back again is to live right unto Jesus like it's our last day to live.

The way that we watch for Jesus coming back again is to study His holy word and apply it to our lives.

The way that we watch for Jesus coming back again is to not deny Jesus before anyone in this world.

The way that we watch for Jesus coming back again is to not be of the world.

Oh, It's Not Me

We can easily believe that, oh it's not me who must be different from anyone else who might not believe every word in the Bible.

We can deny that it's not me who must believe in Jesus Christ for oneself.

We can easily reason that, oh, it's not me who must make my calling very sure about following Jesus all the way over the hot volcano lava of the devil's lies.

We can easily do our own will and believe that, oh, it's not me who Jesus will judge for knowing what is right and not doing it.

We can easily make excuses for wrongdoing and believe that, oh, it's not me who must face up to Jesus on judgment day.

We can break God's Ten Commandments and believe that, oh, it's not me who Jesus will chastised.

We can easily take our health for granted and believe that, oh, it's not me who will get ill.

We can easily disobey God's holy word and believe that, oh, it's not me who will reap what I sow.

We can easily believe that we can say whatever we want to say and believe that, oh, it's not me who the Lord Jesus will hold accountable.

We can easily believe that we can do whatever we want to do and believe that, oh, it's not me who Jesus will cast into hell.

We Will Be Disliked

We will be disliked for standing up for the truth of God's holy word.

We will be disliked by some kinfolks for being different from them because they are not living right unto the Lord.

We will be disliked and a threat to people who don't love the Lord who you and I love.

We will be disliked and criticized for keeping God's Commandments that disobedient people will make excuses not to keep.

We will be disliked and put down for not being like the people of the world.

The people of the world will reject the truth of God's holy word and believe that they will go to heaven after they die.

We will be disliked and despised for not following the crowd on the road that leads to destruction.

Many church folks are on that road and will dislike you and me for following Jesus all the way in His truth that has no errors.

You and I will be disliked for being a true child of God instead of falling for any kind of false doctrines that many church folks are falling for.

We will be disliked for believing in Jesus Christ in our words and body language that goes together for people to see that we truly love Jesus, even though so-called church folks disliked Jesus when He lived on earth without sin.

We will be disliked for not doing what the people of the world love to do.

They will break the holy Sabbath day of rest and criticize you and me for keeping the Sabbath day holy unto the Lord of the Sabbath.

We will be disliked and talked bad about by even so-called Christians for not being like them who would rather believe their own traditions than to believe the Bible truth that is all about our salvation in Jesus Christ from the book of Genesis down to the book of revelations.

Goes to Church

Pride goes to church and can sit down on the church pews to worship self and not Jesus.

Lust goes to church and can sit down on the church pews to worship self and not Jesus.

Covetousness goes to church and can sit down on the church pews to worship self and not Jesus.

Jealousy goes to church and can sit down on the church pews to worship self and not Jesus.

Unforgiveness goes to church and can sit down on the church pews to worship self and not Jesus.

Pretense goes to church and can sit down on the church pews to worship self and not Jesus.

Favoritism goes to church and can sit down on the church pews to worship self and not Jesus.

Selfishness goes to church and can sit down on the church pews to worship self and not Jesus.

Dishonesty goes to church and can sit down on the church pews to worship self and not Jesus.

Discontent goes to church and can sit down on the church pews to worship self and not Jesus.

Evil goes to church and can sit down on the church pews to worship self and not Jesus.

Jesus Christ is the head of the church and sooner or later will cast every evil thing out of the church.

Jesus has His true worshipers in the church where Jesus will cleanse anyone of their sins if there is true repentance in their hearts.

The true children of Jesus go to church and will sit down in the church pews to worship Jesus Christ because they deny self to be true to Jesus.

If You

If you have never been an aircraft pilot you can't relate to someone who is an aircraft pilot.

If you have never been a tractor trailer truck driver you can't relate to a tractor trailer truck driver.

If you have never been a doctor you can't relate to someone who is a doctor.

If you have never been a nurse you can't relate to someone who is a nurse.

If you have never been a soldier you can't relate to someone who is a soldier.

If you have never been a police officer you can't relate to someone who is a police officer.

If you have never been rich, you can't relate to someone who is rich.

If you have never been poor, you can't relate to someone who is poor.

If you have never been in jail, you can't relate to someone who is in jail.

If you have never been sick, you can't relate to someone who is sick.

If you have never been heart broken, you can't relate to someone who has a broken heart.

If you have never been shot, you can't relate to someone who has been shot.

If you have never been married, you can't relate to someone who is married.

If you have never been divorced, you can't relate to someone who is divorced.

If you have never been an author, you can't relate to someone who is an author.

If you have never been a pastor, you can't relate to someone who is a pastor.

If you have never been a musician, you can't relate to someone who is a musician.

If you have never been a teacher, you can't relate to someone who is a teacher.

If you have never been a mechanic, you can't relate to someone who is a mechanic.

If you have never been an actor, you cannot relate to someone who is an actor.

If you have never been a politician, you can't relate to someone who is a politician.

If you have never been a lawyer, you can't relate to someone who is a lawyer.

If you are not a man, you can't relate to another man.

If you are not a woman, you can't relate to another woman.

If you are not an adult, you can't relate to another adult.

If you are not wise, you can't relate to someone who is wise.

If you are not intelligent, you can't relate to someone who is intelligent.

If you are not brilliant, you can't relate to someone who is brilliant.

If you are not good, you can't relate to someone who is good.

If you have never been in love, you can't relate to someone who is in love.

If you can't swim, you can't relate to someone who can swim.

If you have never been an athlete, you can't relate to someone who is an athlete.

If you have never been a publisher, you can't relate to someone who is a publisher.

If you have never been a social worker, you can't relate to someone who is a social worker.

If you have never been a firefighter, you can't relate to someone who is a firefighter.

If you have never been to church, you can't relate to someone who goes to church.

If you don't believe in Jesus Christ, you can't relate to someone who believes in Jesus Christ.

If you don't keep God's Commandments, you can't relate to someone who keeps God's Commandments.

If you are not a Christian, you can't relate to someone who is a Christian.

If your life has never been in danger, you can't relate to someone whose life is in danger.

If you don't read the Bible, you can't relate to someone who reads the Bible.

If you are not content, you can't relate to someone who is content.

If you tell lies, you can't relate to someone who tells the truth.

If you live in lies, you can't relate to someone who lives the truth of God's holy word.

If you have never been a news reporter, you can't relate to someone who is a news reporter.

If you have never been an engineer, you can't relate to someone who is an engineer.

If you have never been a carpenter, you can't relate to someone who is a carpenter.

If you have never been a business owner, you can't relate to someone who is a business owner.

If you have never been disabled, you can't relate to someone who is disabled.

If you have never been in an accident, you can't relate to someone who has been in an accident.

If you have never had any children, you can't relate to someone who has children.

If you have never been homeless, you can't relate to someone who is homeless.

If you don't have a relationship with Jesus Christ, you can't relate to someone who has a relationship with Jesus Christ.

Heaven on Earth

Having peace of mind is heaven on earth.

Being content is heaven on earth.

Treating everybody right is heaven on earth.

Have a good friend is heaven on earth.

Being in good health is heaven on earth.

Believing in Jesus Christ is heaven on earth.

Having a relationship with Jesus Christ is heaven on earth.

Loving Jesus and keeping His Commandments is heaven on earth.

Being a witness of Jesus is heaven on earth.

Giving testimonies about Jesus is heaven on earth.

Being like Jesus is heaven on earth.

Being saved in Jesus is heaven on earth.

Living right unto Jesus is heaven on earth.

Reading God's holy word is heaven on earth.

Understanding God's holy word is heaven on earth.

Being filled with God's Holy Spirit is heaven on earth.

Having faith in Jesus is heaven on earth.

Knowing God's truth is heaven on earth.

Living God's truth is heaven on earth.

Telling the truth is heaven on earth.

Giving Jesus the glory and praise is heaven on earth.

Holding onto Jesus is heaven on earth.

Returning faithful tithes and offerings unto Jesus is heaven on earth.

Worshiping Jesus Christ is heaven on earth.

Trusting Jesus Christ is heaven on earth.
Being blessed by Jesus is heaven on earth.

Waiting on Jesus is heaven on earth.

Praying to Jesus is heaven on earth.

Being humble unto Jesus is heaven on earth.

Giving Jesus our talent is heaven on earth.

Giving Jesus our time is heaven on earth.

Giving Jesus our hearts is heaven on earth.

Confessing and repenting of our sins is heaven on earth.

Living a renewed life in Jesus is heaven on earth.

Giving Jesus all of our burdens is heaven on earth.

Keeping our eyes on Jesus is heaven on earth.

Going to church to assemble ourselves to worship Jesus Christ is heaven on earth.

Too Lightly

Many people will take the Lord too lightly and live their lives like they want to not be in line with God's holy word.

You and I can't afford to take the Lord too lightly, as if He will overlook our excuses for sinning against Him.

Many people will take the Lord too lightly by breaking His commandments like it's a dirty carpet to walk all over.

If we know the truth of God's holy word and don't live by it, then we will take the Lord too lightly and will reap what we sow.

Many people have taken the Lord too lightly and surely regretted it sooner or later in their lives.

You and I should never take the Lord too lightly when the Lord doesn't take saving our souls too lightly.

The Lord is hard on saving as many souls as he can because He shed His blood on the cross and died in our place to save us from our sins and rose from the grave with victory over death.

We must not take the Lord too lightly because that is what the devil wants us to do so that our souls will be lost like he is forever lost for taking the Lord God too lightly.

No one would take their life being in great danger too lightly, but many people will take the Lord too lightly and believe that the Lord can't spare their life from that great danger.

The Lord spares many people's lives from great danger but they still take the Lord too lightly by not thanking the Lord for sparing their lives.

Many people will give thanks to luck or give thanks to a man or woman or boy or girl or an animal for saving their lives from great danger.

Many people will take the Lord too lightly, but to the Lord can use even an animal to save our lives from great danger.

We should never take the Lord too lightly and want the Lord to meet us on our terms to accept what we do wrong that is not in line with God's holy word.

The Lord will never take our souls too lightly and let the devil cause our souls to be lost, because He paid our price on the cross to save us from our sins.

Working Things Out for Us

The Lord is working things out for us when we just don't know how the Lord will bless us.

The Lord is working things out for us when we are sleeping and dreaming away in our beds at night.

The Lord is working things out for us even if some things just don't look good in our lives.

The Lord is working things out for us even when things are going haywire around us.

The Lord is working things out for us when we just don't know what to do.

The Lord is working things out for us when we just don't know what to say.

The Lord is working things out for us when we just don't have a clue how the Lord is working things out for us.

The Lord will especially work things out for all who love Him and keep His Commandments.

The Lord is merciful to even work some things out for people who have turned their backs on Him.

The Lord is working things out for us who don't deserve it, no matter what good things we do.

O Lord, You will always work things out for all of Your children, even unto death that is only a short time to You who is eternal life to raise the righteous dead in the first resurrection when you come back again on the clouds of glory.

O Lord, You are working things out, especially for all of Your children who love and obey You through the good days and bad days in life.

Your Holy Law, O Lord

Your holy law, O Lord, identifies who You are.

No one can separate Your holy law from You, O Lord.

Your holy law is Your character, O Lord.

Your holy law, O Lord, is holy, righteous and perfect like You, O Lord.

O Lord, You are not different from Your holy law.

 Lord, You and Your holy law are the same yesterday, today and tomorrow.

If I break one of Your holy laws, O Lord, I disobey You.

Your holy law, O Lord, is a law of love for You and my neighbors.

Your holy law, O Lord, is who You are.

I must keep Your holy law, O Lord, to be like You who will not break Your own holy law.

O Lord, You are Your holy law and You are grace too.

Through grace, O Lord, I am saved in You.

Your holy law, O Lord, can't save me from my sins.

Only You, O Lord, can save me, and keeping Your holy law, O Lord, lets me know that I am living right unto You.

Keeping Your holy law, O Lord, is my works unto You with my faith in You.

My works and faith unto You go together because You say in Your holy word if I love You I will keep Your Commandments.

O Lord, You would not have given this world Your Commandment laws if it was not necessary to keep in this world.

You kept Your holy law, O Lord, when you lived on earth without sin.

Breaking Your holy law is sinning against You who is holy, righteous and perfect forever and ever.

If I want to be saved in You, O Lord, then I would want to keep Your holy law.

Your holy law, O Lord, will point my sins out to me so I can repent of my sins unto You, my Lord Jesus Christ.

Your holy law, O Lord, is always good for everyone to keep because Your holy law, O Lord, can surely prolong anyone's life unless the Lord allows our lives to be cut short for His reasons that are always right for us.

Is Reality

The truth of Your holy word, O Lord, is reality over all delusional thoughts and words.

The truth of Your holy word, O Lord, is reality over all ignorant thoughts and words.

The truth of Your holy word, O Lord, is reality over every lie.

The truth of Your holy Word, O Lord, is reality over lack of experience.

The truth of Your holy word, O Lord, is reality over feeble-mindedness.

The truth of Your holy word, O Lord, is always real to set anyone free from false beliefs.

The truth of Your holy word, O Lord, is always real to set anyone free from lack of knowledge.

The truth of Your holy word, O Lord, is always real to set anyone free from false impressions.

The truth of Your holy word, O Lord,is always real to set anyone free from being naive.

The truth of Your holy word, O Lord,is always real to set anyone free from deficient intelligence.

The truth of Your holy word, O Lord,is always real and powerful to elevate anyone's mind to think on You, O Lord.

The truth of Your holy word, O Lord, is always real and powerful to convict and convert anyone's soul to seek to find You, O Lord.

The truth of Your holy word, O Lord, is reality to set anyone free from unrealistic dreams.

The truth of Your holy word, O Lord, is reality to set anyone free from unrealistic hopes.

The truth of Your holy word, O Lord, is reality to set anyone free from making the same mistakes over and over again.

The truth of Your holy word, O Lord, is reality to set anyone free from not knowing to believe in You, O Lord, who the demons believe and tremble before You, O Lord.

Will Not Come Easy

Having a relationship with Jesus will not come easy.

We must go through some trials to have a relationship with Jesus.

Having a relationship with Jesus Christ will not come easy because we must go through some hardships to have a relationship with Jesus.

Having a relationship with Jesus will not come easy because we have to deny self to get to know Jesus.

If we don't live the truth of God's holy word, then we don't have a relationship with Jesus.

If we try to please people who are not living right by God's holy word, then we don't have a relationship with Jesus.

Having a relationship with Jesus will not come easy because if we refuse to set the right example before unbelievers, then we don't have a relationship with Jesus.

We must give up all of self to have a relationship with Jesus.

Having a relationship with people can twist and turn up-side down and fail.

Having a relationship with people can be unpredictable.

Having a relationship with people can be difficult.

Having a relationship with people can be questioned.

Having a relationship with people can sometimes come too easy with nothing good behind it.

Having a relationship with Jesus is always a good thing with good things behind it, regardless of going through trials for Jesus' holy name sake.

We will never go through all the hard temptations of the devil who tried to tempt Jesus with everything that he had and failed.

Jesus went through all of the devil's temptations for you and me to have no excuse to not have a relationship with Him.

Jesus came to this world to have a relationship with all men, women, boys and girls who Jesus loves to relate to and save from being lost in sin.

When it comes to relationships, having a relationship with Jesus is the best relationship that we all can have because Jesus will never change on us and will never take us through any changes for the worst, even though having a relationship with Jesus will not come easy.

It's not easy for Jesus to have a relationship with sinners like you and me who can get puffed up with self to relate to the devil.

Let Us Imagine

Let us imagine when Jesus was a little boy.

Jesus must have played with the other little children and said nothing wrong and did nothing wrong to the other little children.

The other little children must have gathered themselves around Jesus who must have talked about His heavenly Father before the other little children.

Jesus must have told them some stories that they listened to with amazement.

Jesus must have played with the other little children and healed them when they fell down and hurt themselves.

Jesus must have told the other little children things that their parents never told them.

Let us imagine when Jesus was a teen-aged boy who had other teen-aged friends.

Jesus was a perfect teen-aged boy who grew up into a perfect man without sin.

The bible says that when Jesus was twelve years old, He talked to very well-educated men who were scholars of religious things.

Those scholars were so amazed by the words of wisdom that Jesus spoke to them.

Let us imagine that the heavenly angels were always camped around Jesus when he was a little boy and a teen-aged boy.

Let us imagine that Jesus understood every little child and every teenager far better than their parents.

Jesus was perfect without sin to know their minds and hearts when he was a little child and became a teen-aged boy.

Let us imagine that Jesus must have amazed every little child and every teenager to want to always be around Him and listen to Him.

Jesus must have talked about nature, the facts of life, and His heavenly Father, God.

Those little children must have told their parents what Jesus told them when Jesus was a little boy.

Those teenagers must have told their parents what Jesus told them when Jesus was a teenager.

Their parents must have been amazed and want to talk to Jesus, who was a sinless little boy and a sinless teenager who had forever more wisdom than King Solomon had.

The little children just didn't know that they were playing with their Creator.

The teenagers didn't know that they were friends with their Creator.

Let us imagine that when Jesus was a little boy, He must have read his parents' minds and knew what they would say and do before they knew what they would say and do, especially in their times of crisis.

Points to Jesus

All of my praise poetry in all of my books points to Jesus Christ, even though some of my poetry has the same title but is written in a different way.

The Holy Spirit is so amazing to inspire me to write different poems with some of them having the same title but different meanings that point to Jesus Christ.

The bible is the same holy book in many nations , and people can read the same bible and get a different meaning that points to Jesus Christ.

Some pastors come up with the same titles to preach their sermons that will have a different meaning but still point people to Jesus Christ.

We all are different and can study the Sabbath school lesson having the same title, but we all can respond to the teacher with a different meaning, but it all points to Jesus Christ.

There are some books that have the same title but are written by different authors writing different words with different meanings that point to Jesus Christ.

Some people in the church have some of the same spiritual gifts, and they can all point people to Jesus Christ in different ways with the same spiritual gifts.

Every true Christian has the same title of a renewed life that points to Jesus Christ, but every Christian will have a different meaning of spiritually maturing through trials that points to Jesus Christ.

Someone asked me if I write the same poems over and over again, and I said no.

I thought about what he asked and I realized that the Holy Spirit inspires me to write the same title for some of my poems, but the meaning is different and will point people to Jesus Christ.

Everybody can have a different meaning about life that has the same title for everybody to live.

Every Christian will have a different meaning relating to their individual experience with Jesus, who is the same title Lord and Savior to everyone who believes in Him to be saved.

You and I can use the same title and give it different meanings.

Jesus Christ is the same title to everyone being filled with His holy spirit giving a different meaning to convictions in everyone's hearts to repent that points to Jesus Christ to forgive us of our sins and save us from our sins.

Made in the USA
Middletown, DE
14 May 2023

30512400R00060